MYTHOLOGY
AROUND THE WORLD

EGYPTIAN
MYTHS

by Eric Braun

Consultant:
Rita Lucarelli
Assistant Professor of Egyptology,
University of California, Berkeley

CAPSTONE PRESS
a capstone imprint

Fact Finders Books are published by Capstone Press,
1710 Roe Crest Drive, North Mankato, Minnesota 56003
www.mycapstone.com

Cataloging-in-publication information is on file with the Library of Congress.
978-1-5157-9603-9 (library binding)
978-1-5157-9617-6 (paperback)
978-1-5157-9610-7 (ebook PDF)

Summary: Make the mythology of ancient Egypt come to life for young readers through engaging
stories and dramatic photos and illustrations. Discover the gods and goddesses behind the myths
and the powers they used to control and change the world. Sidebars, facts, and infographics help
uncover how these myths influenced the culture and daily life of ancient Egypt.

Editorial Credits
Editor: Jennifer Huston
Production Artist: Kazuko Collins
Designer: Russell Griesmer
Media Researcher: Morgan Walters
Production specialist: Kathy McColley

Photo Credits: Alamy: Ivy Close Images, 19, Science History Images, 25; Bridgeman Images: Look
and Learn / Elgar Collection, 7; Depositphotos: vukkostic91, 23; Getty Images: Dorling Kindersley,
11; iStockphoto: Nastasic, (gods) design element throughout; Newscom: akg-images, 29, akg-images/
Rabatti - Domingie, 26, Werner Forman Archive Heritage Images, 13; Shutterstock: AndreyO, 15,
top 16, top left 16, middle left 16, top right 17, Ashwin, 10, BlackMac, 27, Charis Estelle, bottom
16, bottom 17, Denis Krasnoukhov, 6, eFesenko, 5, G.roman, (lightning) 1, cover, Kokhanchikov,
4, Lukasz Szwaj, (paper texture) design element throughout, Madredus, (grunge) design element
throughout, Peter Hermes Furian, 9, photocell, (plate) design element throughout, RaZZeRs, (flare) 1,
cover, T.SALAMATIK, (rain texture) design element throughout, vukkostic91, Cover; Wikimedia:
A. Parrot, middle right 16, Edna R. Russmann, top right 16, Internet Archive Book Images, 21

TABLE OF CONTENTS

CHAPTER 1

THE CULTURE OF ANCIENT EGYPT

Imagine what it was like living in ancient Egypt. Cattle pulled carts in the streets and kicked up dust as they dragged plows in the fields. Because of the scorching sun, growing crops was difficult in some areas.

The Sahara Desert is one of the hottest and driest places on Earth. Summer temperatures in the Sahara are often well over 100 degrees Fahrenheit (38 degrees Celsius).

The Nile is the longest river in the world. It is more than 4,130 miles (6,647 kilometers) long.

As much as possible, ancient Egyptians tried to avoid the Sahara Desert or "red land." With the blazing heat, lack of water, and dangerous creatures, such as snakes and scorpions, this region could be deadly.

The Nile River cuts through the Sahara. Because the Nile was the major source of water in Egypt, most people lived near it in ancient times. The land along the river was also very **fertile**, which made growing crops easier. But life along the Nile had its dangers too, as the river was home to crocodiles and hippos.

fertile—good for growing crops; fertile soil has many nutrients

CYCLE OF FLOODING

Life for the ancient Egyptians centered around the Nile River. Each year by late spring, the Nile was at its lowest level. The land surrounding it was so dry that the earth would crack. But then summertime **monsoons** fed the river, causing it to flood the area nearby. All summer the land was swampy and difficult to live in. When the floodwaters went back down, the soil left behind was perfect for growing crops.

When the Nile River reached its lowest levels, the land around it became extremely dry.

Men ride camels across the water-soaked land following the flooding of the Nile.

The ancient Egyptians could not always depend on the floods, though. Some years the floods didn't come at all. Other times the floods were too small. When there wasn't enough water for the crops to grow, many people died from lack of food.

Some years the floods were too big and destructive. Even so, to the people of ancient Egypt, the floods were a gift from the heavens. They believed the floods **symbolized** the coming of the god Hapi, a god of water and **fertility**.

monsoon—very heavy rainfall
symbolize—to stand for or represent something else
fertility—the ability to support the growth of many plants

Kingdoms, Pharaohs, and Priests

By about 3400 BC, two kingdoms had been established in ancient Egypt. Lower Egypt, where the Nile **Delta** was located, was in the north. The other kingdom, called Upper Egypt, was located south of Lower Egypt. Around 3150 BC, King Menes of Upper Egypt conquered Lower Egypt and **united** the two kingdoms.

With the kingdoms united, Menes wanted to form one national religion. The ancient Egyptians believed in many gods and goddesses—some even had the same characteristics and duties. Some of them were national and official gods that were worshipped in huge temples. Others were local gods that were only worshipped in certain towns.

In ancient Egypt **pharaohs** were the only humans who could communicate with the gods. Priests took care of the temples where the gods were worshipped. Priests were also in charge of religious **rituals**. For example, they put perfume or food on the statues of the gods inside the temples.

delta—the triangle-shaped area where a river deposits mud, sand, and pebbles

unite—to join together to make a whole

pharaoh—a ruler of ancient Egypt

ritual—an action that is always performed in the same way, usually as part of a religious or social ceremony

ANCIENT EGYPT

Upper and Lower Egypt were named because the Nile flows from south to north. Therefore, the upper part of the river is in the south and the lower part is in the north.

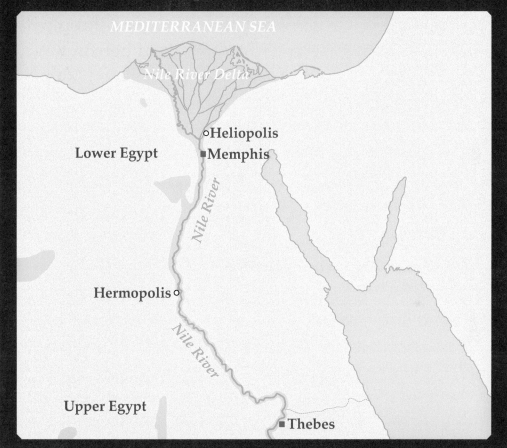

DID YOU KNOW?

The word *pharaoh* comes from the ancient Egyptian word *per-aa*, which means "great house." Today we use the word *pharaoh* to mean a king or ruler in ancient Egypt.

ANCIENT EGYPTIAN WAY OF LIFE—AND DEATH

Women in Egypt had the same legal rights as men. They could run businesses and buy and sell property. There were even female rulers, such as Hatshepsut and Cleopatra, who shaped the politics and religion of the country.

Ancient Egyptians were responsible for many of the world's earliest technical advances. They invented a type of thick paper called **papyrus** as well as levers and ramps. They also made great advances in math and astronomy. By counting dates on the calendar, they could predict when the Nile would flood. In doing so they made improvements in agriculture, for example, **irrigating** crops on a large scale.

The ancient Egyptians also made important developments in medicine. For example, they recognized the importance of washing regularly to avoid diseases.

Cleopatra ruled Egypt in the 1st century BC.

The ancient Egyptians used log rollers and ramps to move heavy materials when building large structures, such as the pyramids.

The ancient Egyptians were also expert shipbuilders, and their art and architecture was known for its details and beauty. Much of their art had to do with the idea of death. To them, life on Earth was only a small part of an endless journey. For that reason, pharaohs were buried with weapons, furniture, food, and other items—anything they might need in the afterlife.

Did You Know?

Pharaohs were considered earthly versions of Horus, the first national god and the son of Osiris. Horus was the god of the sky, war, and hunting.

papyrus—a type of paper made from a tall grasslike plant in ancient times

irrigate—to supply water to dry soil through methods such as pipes and channels

CHAPTER 2

THE CREATION OF THE WORLD AND THE GODS

People from Upper and Lower Egypt had their own beliefs about the creation of the world. There were four major creation myths and some minor ones. They were all narrated and illustrated on monuments and on papyrus.

All Egyptian creation stories had certain things in common. They told of the gods' births and connected them through a family structure. The stories also put the Nile Valley at the center of all creation.

FROM DARK WATER COMES THE UNIVERSE

Ancient Egyptians believed that life was an endless journey that began with the creation of the universe. The best-known creation story came from the city of Heliopolis. According to this story, before the universe was created there was nothing but endless water that was dark and silent. This endless water was called Nun, and the Egyptians came to worship it as the first god. A hill rose out of the water. On the hill was Atum, who would become king of the gods. Atum set in motion the creation of the universe. He made the Benben—the mound of creation. This was the first piece of dry land, and the people believed it was the center of Heliopolis.

When Atum sneezed, out came two children. Shu was the god of air, and Tefnut was the goddess of moisture. Shu and Tefnut had two children—the earth, called Geb, and the sky, called Nut. Geb and Nut had two sons, Osiris and Seth, and two daughters, Isis and Nephthys.

This painting shows a scene from one creation story. In it, Shu holds up Nut (the sky), keeping her separate from Geb (the earth).

DID YOU KNOW?

In ancient Egyptian myths, it was common for gods and goddesses to marry their siblings.

OTHER CREATION MYTHS

Another major creation myth came from the town of Hermopolis. In this story, the first eight gods were snakes and frogs in a dark ocean. They swam around in pairs until suddenly they came together as one, forming the sun god Amun-Ra. From the water came the mound of creation. The people of Hermopolis believed the mound was in the center of their city.

The Egyptian city of Memphis was the source of another creation myth, this one focusing on a god called Ptah. Ptah was first a dark ocean that existed before anything else—like Nun from the Heliopolis story. When Ptah described something, it appeared. In this myth Ptah also created the gods and goddesses described in the creation stories from Heliopolis and Hermopolis.

Much later the last of the four major creation myths was developed in the city of Thebes. In this version Amun was combined with Ra to become Amun-Ra. He was the sole creator of the world. Amun-Ra chose Khnum, a local Thebes god, to create humans. Khnum used a special clay from the banks of the Nile to mold human bodies. Then he inserted organs, such as hearts and lungs, into the bodies. After wrapping it all in skin, he breathed life into humans.

According to the creation story of Thebes, Khnum (shown here) was the creator of humankind.

 ATUM was the king of the gods and the creator of the universe.

 SHU was the god of air and held up the sky.

 TEFNUT was the goddess of moisture. She also represented the moon and the sun.

 GEB was the god of the earth. He was also the brother of Nut.

 NUT was the goddess of the sky and the mother of several major gods, including Osiris and Isis.

 OSIRIS became god of the Underworld— the land of the dead—after his death.

 ISIS, the sister and wife of Osiris, was the most powerful goddess.

 SETH, the brother of Osiris, was the god of the desert and storms. Later, he also became the god of chaos and war.

THE MAJOR EGYPTIAN GODS AND GODDESSES

Over time, many of the important Egyptian stories and gods were combined. Several of these gods were worshipped throughout the nation. The most well-known gods and goddesses played important roles in Egyptian myths.

 HORUS was worshipped throughout Egypt in different forms, often as a sky god. Images showed him with the head of a falcon and the sun for one eye and the moon for the other.

 MAAT was a goddess who symbolized truth, order, and justice as well as harmony and balance. She was often pictured with the feather of truth.

 RA, the god of the sun, represented warmth, light, and growth. Ra was usually pictured in human form with a falcon head and the sun for a crown.

 NEPHTHYS was the goddess of death and mourning and a protector of mummies and the dead.

 ANUBIS was the god of the dead and the protector of lost souls. He is often shown with the head of a dog and the body of a man.

CHAPTER 3

THE STORIES

The Egyptians created myths to help them understand how the natural world worked. Some myths taught lessons about right and wrong. One of the most important myths was the story of how Osiris was killed by his brother. This story explained several important areas of Egyptian life.

OSIRIS AND SETH

The ancient Egyptians believed that the earliest gods lived among the people and ruled them like kings. As a wise and powerful ruler, Osiris gave people laws and knowledge of farming. He showed them how to live peacefully in their villages. During Osiris' reign, crops were healthy, food was plentiful, and people were treated equally. Because the Egyptian people adored Osiris, his brother, Seth, became very jealous. One night Seth went into Osiris' room while he was sleeping and measured his brother's body. Then he used the measurements to build a beautiful wooden chest.

When Seth threw a big party, he brought out the chest for the final game of the night. Everyone had to take turns trying to fit inside the box. The person who best fit into the box would get to keep it.

One by one, guests climbed into the chest, and none of them fit inside. Finally Osiris climbed into the chest, and it fit him perfectly. With Osiris inside, Seth slammed the lid and sealed it shut. Then he threw the chest into the Nile.

Seth (lower right) brings out a wooden chest to see which of his guests best fit inside. He knows that his brother, Osiris (standing, in white), will be the winner.

When Isis heard what had happened to Osiris, she rushed to the riverbank to find the wooden chest. After searching for days, Isis located the box. When she opened it, she found her husband's dead body inside. Isis hid Osiris' body in the grass so Seth would not find it. Then she went to get her sister, Nephthys, so they could perform a ritual to bring Osiris back to life.

But Seth did find Osiris' body. And when he did, he cut his brother's body into 14 pieces and threw them all over Egypt. When Isis returned and found her husband gone, she used her magical powers to turn herself into a bird. Then she flew around the country until she found all the pieces. After she had all the pieces, Isis and her sister, Nephthys, stitched Osiris back together and wrapped him in linens like a mummy. Finally, with the help of Nephthys, Isis used her magical powers to bring Osiris back to life.

The sun god Ra told Osiris that he would not remain among the living. Although Osiris had taught humans many important things, Ra said he had to go to the Underworld and become its king. This meant Osiris would judge the dead and send them to the Field of Reeds if they were worthy. The Field of Reeds was the ancient Egyptians' concept of heaven.

Isis (right) and Nephthys (left) perform a ritual to bring Osiris back to life.

But who would become king of the living in Egypt? Of course, Seth wanted the throne for himself. But Isis was pregnant with Osiris' son, Horus, who would become king. After Horus was born, Isis hid him away until he was a man. When Horus confronted Seth, they battled each other. In some versions of the story, Horus killed Seth. In others, Osiris told Seth he would have beasts from the Underworld attack him unless he gave up. Seth did. In both stories Horus became the king of Egypt.

This story explained how Osiris became king of the Underworld. With Osiris as the king of the dead, Egyptians no longer had reason to fear death. They trusted Osiris to guide them and take care of them as long as they had led good lives. This myth also explained why the pharaohs were treated as **descendants** of the gods. The pharaohs' power came from the gods, so to disobey a pharaoh was to go against the gods.

descendants—all the relatives who trace their family roots back to one person

Horus (left) battles his uncle, Seth, to become king of the gods.

Did You Know?

The sun god Ra was said to be a child in the early morning, a man at noon, and an old man in the evening. Each day he traveled across the sky and the Underworld, making the sun rise and set. He made his way through the Underworld during the night and was reborn at dawn. For the Egyptians, this myth explained the cycles of day and night.

Isis and the Seven Scorpions

After Osiris went to the Underworld, Isis hid from Seth to keep her unborn baby safe. She decided that the safest thing to do was to keep traveling. As Isis walked, she kept quiet and avoided attention. Along the journey seven poisonous scorpions protected her.

One day while the group was walking, Isis grew very tired. She stopped at the home of a rich woman to ask for a place to stay. But the woman saw the scorpions and slammed the door on them. The scorpions were furious. Later that evening Isis and the scorpions stopped at the home of a poor girl who let them stay with her. But the scorpions were still angry, so they put all their poison into one scorpion. That scorpion went to the home of the rich woman. There, it stung the woman's young son.

When the rich woman ran into town looking for help for her little boy, Isis heard her cries. She could not bear to let the boy suffer and die, so she used her magical powers to save him.

The rich woman was so grateful that she gave all she owned to the poor girl who had helped Isis. For the ancient Egyptians, this myth taught an important lesson about being kind to strangers.

IMHOTEP

Some myths were created about real people. Imhotep was a philosopher, priest, and talented architect who worked for the second pharaoh, Djoser. When Djoser asked him to build a **tomb**, Imhotep built the first pyramid, the Step Pyramid at Saqqara. It was larger than previous tombs, and it was safer from grave robbers. Because of Imhotep's creation, many more pyramids were later built.

After Imhotep died, myths were told about him. According to one myth, he was the son of Ptah, the creator god from the Memphis tradition.

tomb—a room or building that holds a dead body and any items that were buried with that person

CHAPTER 4

JUSTICE AND THE END OF LIFE

The ancient Egyptians thought about death often and were very aware that life on Earth was short. The Egyptians believed that everything in the universe was in a constant balance without end. People were also part of this constant and eternal balance. If a person lived life in tune with Maat, that person would have a good life and find peace in the afterlife.

Egyptians believed that after death, each deceased person traveled a dangerous journey through the Underworld. There, lakes of fire, demons, and other dangers awaited. Maps and spells helped prepare souls for this journey.

At the core of all Egyptian myths is the concept, or idea, of Maat. Maat was not just an idea but also a goddess.

THE BOOK OF THE DEAD

Much of what we know about Egyptian beliefs of death and the afterlife comes from copies of *The Book of the Dead*. This book of spells helped guide dead people through the afterlife. They needed to know where to go, how to avoid demons, and what prayers to say, among other things. *The Book of the Dead* helped dead people on their journey.

Early on, these spells were recorded in paintings and **hieroglyphs** on the walls of tombs and coffins. Then they were written on papyrus and buried with bodies.

For centuries only the king could reach eternal life with the help of the book and its magical spells. But later on the book was seen as so important that anyone could get one—assuming they could afford to have a scribe make them a copy. The more money you had, the more complete the book would be and the more spells it would include.

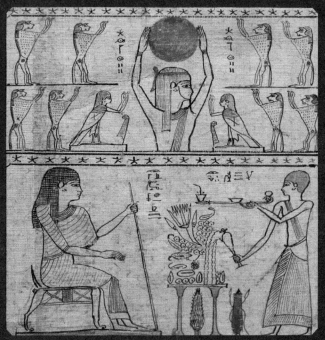

a drawing from *The Book of the Dead*

hieroglyph—a picture or symbol used in the ancient Egyptian system of writing

The Weighing of the Heart

If a dead person reached the Hall of Truth, he or she met Osiris. Osiris weighed the dead person's heart on a scale against Maat's feather of truth. If the heart was heavier than the feather, then it was heavy with sin. If this happened, the dead person would not receive eternal life. If the heart was lighter than the feather, Osiris consulted Thoth, the god of wisdom, and 42 other gods. Dead people that were judged worthy were allowed to pass through the hall into the Field of Reeds. There, the dead person was given back everything he or she had lost during life to enjoy for all eternity.

Continuation of Maat

Even though the world was based on Maat, evil and chaos still existed within it. The name for this evil and chaos was Isfet. The ancient Egyptians believed Maat and Isfet had to balance each other out for the world to be stable.

The end of the world was not described in detail in Egyptian texts. However, Atum said he would one day return the world to its original state in the dark waters of Nun. After that only Atum, Osiris, and Maat would continue to exist. This left the possibility that a new world could arise from the waters just as the old one had.

PREPARING THE BODY

In order to reach the afterlife, ancient Egyptians believed that the body must be preserved. They did this through **mummification**, a process that could take up to 10 weeks.

Ancient Egyptian priests mummify a body.

To prepare the body for mummification, special priests removed the internal organs. Then the body was dried using a type of salt. Next the body was rubbed with perfumed oils and wrapped with strips of cloth.

Egyptians began to mummify their dead around 2600 BC. The practice was continued for more than 2,000 years. Professionals charged different prices depending on the quality of their services. More money meant better mummification, which would keep the body preserved longer. In modern times, well-preserved mummies that are thousands of years old have been found throughout Egypt.

mummification—the process of preserving a dead body with special salts and cloth to make it last for a very long time

GLOSSARY

delta (DEL-tuh)—the triangle-shaped area where a river deposits mud, sand, and pebbles

descendants (di-SEN-duhnts)—all the relatives who trace their family roots back to one person

fertile (FUHR-tuhl)—good for growing crops; fertile soil has many nutrients

fertility (FUHR-til-uh-tee)—the ability to support the growth of many plants

hieroglyph (HYE-ruh-glif)—a picture or symbol used in the ancient Egyptian system of writing

irrigate (IHR-uh-gate)—to supply water to dry soil through methods such as pipes and channels

monsoon (mon-SOON)—very heavy rainfall

mummification (muh-mi-fuh-KAY-shun)—the process of preserving a dead body with special salts and cloth to make it last for a very long time

papyrus (puh-PYE-ruhss)—a type of paper made from a tall grasslike plant in ancient times

pharaoh (FAIR-oh)—a ruler of ancient Egypt

ritual (RICH-oo-uhl)—an action that is always performed in the same way, usually as part of a religious or social ceremony

symbolize (SIM-buh-lize)—to stand for or represent something else

tomb (TOOM)—a room or building that holds a dead body and any items that were buried with that person

unite (yoo-NITE)—to join together to make a whole

READ MORE

Conklin, Wendy, and Blane Conklin. *You Are There! Ancient Egypt 1336 BC.* Huntington Beach, Calif.: Teacher Created Materials, 2017.

Napoli, Donna Jo. *Treasury of Egyptian Mythology: Classic Stories of Gods, Goddesses, Monsters & Mortals.* Washington, D.C.: National Geographic, 2013.

Owings, Lisa. *What We Get from Egyptian Mythology.* Mythology and Culture. Ann Arbor, Mich.: Cherry Lake Publishing, 2015.

INTERNET SITES

Use FactHound to find Internet sites related to this book.

Visit www.facthound.com

Just type in 9781515796039 and go.

 Check out projects, games and lots more at
www.capstonekids.com

CRITICAL THINKING QUESTIONS

1. The Greek gods were often jealous, angry, and cruel. Why do you think they acted this way? Use details from the text in your answer.

2. What lessons do you think the story "Isis and the Seven Scorpions" (page 24) taught Egyptians? Are those lessons still important today? Why or why not?

3. Maat, the goddess of truth, justice, and order, was also the most important concept to ancient Egyptians. What do you think is the most important concept in your community? Create a god or goddess to represent it.

INDEX